embroidery

The COUNTRYLIVING Needlework Collection

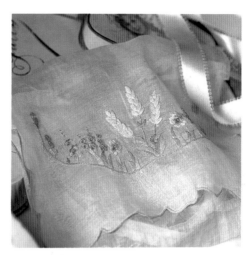

embroidery

projects · techniques · motifs

Karen Elder

Photography by Pia Tryde

Quadrille

page 1: Blue-and-white Bedspread (see page 54)
page 2: Cutwork Leaves (see page 40)
page 3: Handkerchief Sachet (see page 70)
page 5: Embroidered Buttons (see page 88)

Detail photography • Peter Cassidy, Dave King
Illustrations • Kate Simunek

First published in 1995 by
Quadrille Publishing Limited
27–31 Charing Cross Road, London WC2H 0LS

This paperback edition first published in 1998

Published in association with the National Magazine Company Limited
Country Living is a trademark of the National Magazine Company Limited

Publishing Director • Anne Furniss
Art Director • Mary Evans
Managing Editor • Jane O'Shea
Editor • Patsy North
Copy Editor • Sarah Widdicombe
Art Editor • Jo Tapper
Production Assistant • Kate Walford

British Library Cataloguing-in-Publication Data
A catalogue record for this book is available
from the British Library.

ISBN 1 899988 57 2

Printed and bound in Spain

contents

Introduction

The joy of embroidery – the embellishment of fabric with stitching – lies not only in the finished work but also in the hours of pleasure involved in the execution of even the smallest piece. The dictionary describes embroidery as 'inessential ornament' – a brutal description, for without embroidery the world would be a poorer place. Before the relatively recent availability of printed cloth and sophisticated weaves, the only means to decorate textiles was often embroidery. The dictionary is not so dismissive of painting, for the entry reads 'representing or depicting by colours on a surface', but this could equally well apply to embroidery, for stitches are like the strokes of a pencil, pen or brush in drawing and painting. Perhaps embroidery's most exciting quality is its ability to fit any shape, almost without compromise. Next comes the notion that every embroiderer is making something unique and that no two pieces of work will ever be the same – invaluable in this age of mass production.

Much beautiful embroidery is even, fine, counted and 'perfect'. However, the approach taken in this book is to free the mind and fingers a little to explore the possibilities of stitches, colour, texture and personal expression, rather than to focus on stitch perfection – evenness of stitches improves with practice.

The term 'embroidery' encompasses many types of decoration of textiles, usually using a needle and some form of thread, bead or sequin. For this book, the more specialized forms, such as canvaswork, goldwork and counted stitch work (except one piece of counted cross stitch) have been omitted in favour of providing a general grounding in free-style embroidery. The fifteen relatively straightforward projects use a simple stitch library easily accessible to anyone wishing to learn. Once these stitches have been mastered, you will be able to move on to more ambitious projects without difficulty; in the meantime, this approach demonstrates that fancy and highly skilled workmanship is not always necessary to produce an effective, pretty or impressive piece of work. In fact, many of the designs in this book use only one or two stitches.

It is often thought that large doses of patience and skill are necessary to be a successful embroiderer, but it can be argued that patience is only needed for tedious work, which hardly applies to most embroidery. With a few easily learned stitches, much pleasure can be drawn from the process as well as from the finished piece.

Before you start

There is a vast array of fabrics, threads, needles, scissors, embroidery frames and accessories available, which may appear daunting to the novice. Most of these materials and tools are designed with specific purposes in mind, so follow the guidelines provided in this chapter, and also take the advice of your needlework supplier to select the right products for the projects you wish to make.

However, it is possible to use a huge variety of fabrics and threads that are not specifically designed for embroidery. Once you have explored techniques a little, and acquired some knowledge of how the various materials behave, you will be well equipped to choose the right weight of fabric for the thread, and a needle that will do a good job.

It is also interesting to look at traditional embroidery from different parts of the world, where local materials may be all that are available: roughly woven, brightly coloured fabrics form the background to many ethnic designs. Embroidery is an integral part of the lives of many quite primitive communities, as it is the only way they have of adorning their clothes. There is a lot we can learn from their uninhibited approach.

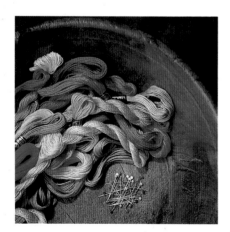

materials & equipment

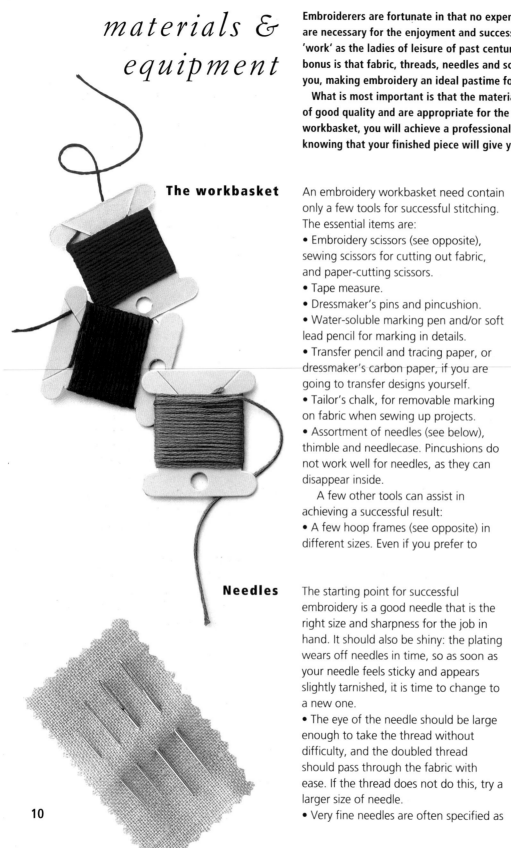

Embroiderers are fortunate in that no expensive or space-taking materials or equipment are necessary for the enjoyment and successful execution of a piece of stitching, or 'work' as the ladies of leisure of past centuries were so fond of calling it. The added bonus is that fabric, threads, needles and scissors are easy and light to take around with you, making embroidery an ideal pastime for travelling and holidays.

What is most important is that the materials and equipment selected for a project are of good quality and are appropriate for the task. With the right items in your workbasket, you will achieve a professional-looking result and have the satisfaction of knowing that your finished piece will give you pleasure for many years.

The workbasket

An embroidery workbasket need contain only a few tools for successful stitching. The essential items are:
• Embroidery scissors (see opposite), sewing scissors for cutting out fabric, and paper-cutting scissors.
• Tape measure.
• Dressmaker's pins and pincushion.
• Water-soluble marking pen and/or soft lead pencil for marking in details.
• Transfer pencil and tracing paper, or dressmaker's carbon paper, if you are going to transfer designs yourself.
• Tailor's chalk, for removable marking on fabric when sewing up projects.
• Assortment of needles (see below), thimble and needlecase. Pincushions do not work well for needles, as they can disappear inside.
    A few other tools can assist in achieving a successful result:
• A few hoop frames (see opposite) in different sizes. Even if you prefer to

work without a frame, there are times when it is a necessity – for example, when working large areas of satin stitch and other long stitches. French knots, too, are difficult to work without a frame. The work can be mounted on to a hoop in seconds.
• Thread bobbins. These are also extremely practical, for however carefully embroidery skeins are used, they can easily get tangled as the threads are withdrawn. Winding the thread on to a cardboard bobbin can save time and energy, and avoid frustration. Write the colour number on the card for future reference.
• Magnifying glass that can hang around your neck. This will keep your hands free and is helpful not only for those with less-than-perfect eyesight, but also for working very small stitches, like the ones used in the Embroidered Buttons on page 88.

Needles

The starting point for successful embroidery is a good needle that is the right size and sharpness for the job in hand. It should also be shiny: the plating wears off needles in time, so as soon as your needle feels sticky and appears slightly tarnished, it is time to change to a new one.
• The eye of the needle should be large enough to take the thread without difficulty, and the doubled thread should pass through the fabric with ease. If the thread does not do this, try a larger size of needle.
• Very fine needles are often specified as

they run through the fabric with ease, but for those with less nimble fingers they can be difficult to hold. Often a slightly larger one may be substituted successfully.
• Needles are often sold in packs of mixed sizes, allowing for some experimentation.
• Needle sizes are denoted by numbers: the lower the number, the larger the needle, so a size 1 needle is larger than a size 2, and so on.
    The four types of needles used for embroidery are discussed opposite, but ultimately the choice is yours.

Crewel (embroidery) needles come in sizes 1 to 10. They have sharp points to pierce the fabric easily, and long eyes to take one or more threads of stranded cotton or wool. These are the needles used for most embroidery projects. Apart from the long eye, they are the same in length and point as ordinary sewing (Sharps) needles.

Tapestry needles come in sizes 13 to 24. They have rounded, blunt ends which slip between the warp and weft of fabrics such as blockweave and heavy evenweaves for counted embroidery (see page 15) without splitting them and, as the name suggests, are ideal for use on needlepoint canvas, where a sharp point would catch. The oval-shaped eyes are generous in size to allow thick yarns to be threaded.

Chenille needles are identical to tapestry needles except for their sharp point. They are used for fabrics like twill and for thicker yarns that may not thread into a crewel (embroidery) needle.

Betweens (quilting needles) come in sizes 1 to 12. They are sharp ended and short, for quick, even stitching such as running stitch, backstitch and stem stitch. They are also good for French knots, being easy to manipulate.

Scissors

A pair of small, really sharp, pointed scissors is an essential tool for every embroiderer. The blades should be sharp all the way along, especially at the point. A larger pair of scissors for cutting fabric is also necessary.

Embroidery frames

Hoops
For most kinds of embroidery a round tambour frame, or embroidery 'hoop' as it is usually called, is a simple, cheap but useful tool. It consists of two wooden hoops that fit inside one another; the fabric is stretched over the smaller hoop and then the larger one is fitted over the top and a screw on the larger hoop is used to adjust the tension. A hoop helps keep the fabric smooth and the stitches flat, especially where long stitches, such as satin stitch, need to be made.
• If the area of embroidery is not too large, use a hoop into which the whole design will fit. On larger pieces, the hoop can be moved around.
• Always remove the hoop when you have finished working, as it can stretch and mark the fabric if left on between stitching sessions.
   • A hoop holds the work much more evenly if the smaller hoop is bound with cloth. Wrap strips of sheeting or bias binding all around the edge and finish off with a few stitches to hold it in place. The embroidery fabric will then sit more comfortably in the frame.
• Hoops are also available that can be screwed to a table, or with a stand that you can sit on, leaving both hands free to work. The right hand is kept under the hoop and the left hand on top (vice versa for left-handed stitchers); with a little practice, this is a quicker way to work. The range of holders and stands for hoops and frames is too vast to explore in detail here, but the most important feature of any type of stand is that it holds the work firmly and does not wobble when in use.

Rectangular frames
If you like to work with a frame, large pieces of embroidery are best mounted on to a rectangular frame. Machine stitch a piece of webbing or tough fabric around the edge of the fabric to be worked on, and then lace or stitch this on to the frame, depending on its design. This will take the main stress points away from the embroidery fabric, preventing it from distorting.

11

Thread

Just about any yarn may be used for embroidery, providing it can be threaded through a needle and a suitable fabric found for it – doubtless soft string would embroider well on sackcloth. However, until you have used a few different types of yarn it is as well to stick to the proprietary embroidery threads that are tried and tested for strength and colourfastness. It would be a pity to spend many hours plying your needle, only to find that the thread was not strong enough for the job or that the colours ran when washed or dampened for pressing (see page 20).

Threads are packaged in many different types of skein and hank. Some are wound so that lengths can be pulled out easily, as in stranded cotton. However, many need the skein bands removed and the yarn untwisted or unfolded before they can be used. These types, for example pearl cotton and coton à broder (see page 14), often fall out into a skein that can be cut at each end to create a bundle of thread the right length for stitching. If you knot the bundle loosely in the centre, it will keep tidy and will not tangle. Do not use elastic bands to hold strands together as they spoil the thread.

A stitch can take on a very different appearance when worked in different threads. Try out a variety of thicknesses of thread in one stitch to see the effects. Some are much easier in finer yarns, but the boldness of thick corded threads can create a dramatic impact.

Stranded cotton

The most commonly used embroidery thread is stranded cotton. It is sometimes referred to as 'embroidery silk' as it has a silky sheen, and it can sometimes be difficult to tell at a glance whether real silk or stranded cotton has been used for a particular piece.

Stranded cotton is widely available in several hundred colours. It is usually made up of six fine strands that can be separated to create different thicknesses of thread.

Pearl cotton (coton perlé)

This thread has a lustrous, corded finish and, in contrast to stranded cotton, the strands cannot be separated. It is, however, available in four different gauges – 3, 5, 8 and 12 – 3 being the thickest.

Stranded silk

Stranded silk threads are similar to stranded cotton in their thickness and composition, and can be used for the same purposes.

Coton à broder (broder spécial)

This is a single-thread mercerized cotton with a slight sheen. It is especially suitable for cutwork, where stranded threads may not pull through evenly on close buttonhole stitching.

Soft embroidery cotton

This relatively thick, single-thread yarn has a matt finish. It is best used on loose-weave fabrics, as it is difficult to pull through tightly woven ones and can look lumpy unless a suitable stitch is chosen, such as French knots.

Fine embroidery cotton (flower thread)

Fine embroidery cotton is similar to coton à broder except that it has a matt finish as opposed to a sheen.

Crewel wool or Persian yarn

These are the wool yarns most commonly used for surface embroidery. They are both fine threads that can be used either singly or stranded together, as required. Crewel wool comes as a single thread and persian yarn comes with three threads together, which can be separated.

Knitting wool

Some fine knitting wools – for example, two-ply Botany wool – can also be used for embroidery, but care should be taken to ensure that it is good quality, 100% wool, and colourfast.

Other threads

There are also metallic threads, space-dyed yarns, and numerous varieties of silk, cotton, and synthetic threads available. Once you have mastered the basic stitches, experimenting with these can bring individuality to your work and is also rewarding in itself.

Fabrics The main characteristic of specially produced embroidery fabrics is the evenness of the weave in both directions, where threads or blocks of threads per 2.5cm (1in) are quoted in the fabric description. This is known as the 'count'. These fabrics are divided into two main groups:

• **Blockweave** fabrics have the warp and weft threads grouped to create a box-like structure, making it very easy to follow a cross stitch chart. Each stitch is worked over one block, or square, of the fabric. The finished size of the piece can thus be calculated with great accuracy. The most widely used blockweave fabric is Aida, which is available in a variety of weights, counts and fibres to suit many uses. Most commonly used for cross stitch, Aida fabric is also suitable for most kinds of geometric patterning.

• **Evenweave** fabrics have, as the name suggests, the same number of warp and weft threads per square centimetre (inch). When working cross stitch on evenweaves, the crosses are usually made over two threads in each direction; for other stitches in counted work, the number of threads over which each stitch must carry is usually indicated in the pattern. The finished size of a design can then be calculated fairly easily when working from a chart on a specified count of fabric. Evenweaves are the best fabrics to choose for pulled thread work and drawn thread work, and also for Hardanger work – a counted satin stitch cutwork technique – all of which are unsuitable for blockweave fabrics.

Choosing fabrics

All these embroidery fabrics are available in good needlework shops. However, the choice need not be restricted to these; many other good-quality fabrics are suitable for embroidery, and this is demonstrated in the projects in this book. The choice of fabric is dependent on the type of embroidery, the chosen yarn and the use to which the finished item will be put, these factors determining the looseness of the weave, the degree of texture in relation to the thread, and the durability and washability of the fabric. As a general rule, heavy yarns are unsuitable for very fine fabrics, and fine yarns may be lost on a heavy or textured cloth.

preparation

Time taken in preparing a piece of fabric for embroidery is time well spent. Placing the design with care, transferring the pattern using the most suitable method and ensuring that you have the right equipment can save trouble in the long run. It is also worth experimenting with pattern markers to ensure that the pattern transfers clearly on to the chosen fabric, and that it will wash out properly if required. Always press your fabric before starting, so that you have a smooth, flat surface on which to work.

Preparing fabric

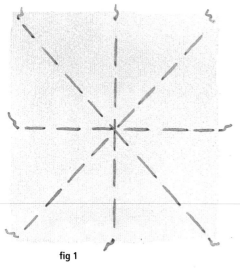

fig 1

The first step when embarking on a new piece of embroidery is to plan the placement of the design.

• Finding and marking the centre of the fabric is necessary for both geometric and free-form patterns. To do this, fold the fabric in half and tack along the crease. Fold the fabric the other way and tack along the intersecting crease, so that the fabric is divided into four rectangles of the same size.

• To mark where corners should turn for rectangles, make two further folds in the fabric, this time diagonally, and tack the creases as before (fig 1).

Within this framework it is simple to lay out symmetrical and formal patterns,

while freestyle designs and motifs are easier to place if these axes are marked.

• Oversew the edges of the fabric or cover them with masking tape before starting to stitch to prevent loose, frayed threads catching in the work. However, only use masking tape if you are going to trim the edge right off. The glue will mark the fabric.

• Once the design has been chosen, it may be necessary to enlarge or reduce it in size to fit the project for which it is intended. This is now a simple process, if carried out on a photocopier – a good copying shop will be able to do the calculations for you to make your chosen design a specific size.

Transferring patterns

To transfer the design on to your fabric, you will need to use a method that is sympathetic to the work.

• For easily washed embroidery, tracing (method 1) is a good choice.

• If the fabric is too thick for the pattern to be traceable through it, dressmaker's carbon (method 2) is a good alternative, as the marks will wash out.

• If the embroidery will cover the markings completely, then making an iron-on transfer (method 3) creates the clearest image.

Whichever method you choose, be sure to transfer the whole pattern before starting to stitch, for once stitching has begun it is difficult to lay the fabric flat. In addition, the placement of free-form designs will become difficult to judge and symmetrical designs will become distorted and may not join up successfully if marked out piecemeal.

Method 1: tracing

The simplest and often most successful method on thin fabrics is to trace the pattern on directly using a water-soluble pen or very fine pencil. The problem with the latter is that the lead can make the embroidery thread dirty. However, any dirt should wash out, except on very pale colours. Water-soluble pen markings can fade away before the embroidery is finished, but are fine for small projects.

1 Draw or trace the design on to a piece of tracing or thin white paper and tape it to a window.

2 Tape the fabric on top and trace the pattern on to it.

Method 2: dressmaker's carbon paper

This special fabric carbon comes in packs of three different colours, so choose one that will be clearly visible on your fabric. The drawback is that the markings may brush off before the embroidery is finished. Pressing will prevent this, but the markings will then be permanent.

1 Draw, trace or photocopy the pattern you wish to transfer.

2 Place the fabric on a clean, flat surface and tape it down using masking tape.

3 Place the carbon paper face down on the fabric and tape to secure.

4 Place the pattern on top and tape it down. Using a ballpoint pen, trace carefully around the pattern.

5 Turn up one corner to see if the design has transferred successfully before removing the paper. Try not to lean on the carbon with your hand as it may smudge on to the fabric.

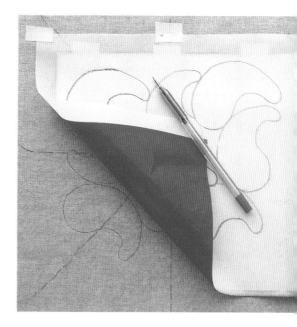

Method 3: making a transfer

Special transfer pencils are available for transferring embroidery patterns, but on many fabrics they do not work well. Synthetic fabrics and those with a finish or dressing work best, but the problem can be overcome by giving other fabrics a thorough spraying with spray starch just before transferring the pattern. Test the transfer pencil on a small piece of the fabric before using. Transfer pencil may not wash out, so it is only suitable where the embroidery covers the marking fully.

1 Trace the design on to a sheet of thin tracing paper.

2 Turn the tracing over and trace the back using the transfer pencil.

3 Press the fabric that you wish to use, spray well with starch if it has no dressing on it, and then pin on the transfer (transfer-pencil side down) and press slowly using a hot iron (do not use a steam setting).

4 Turn up one corner to see if the design has transferred successfully before unpinning the paper.

from start to finish

Threading the needle, positioning the first stitch, and starting and finishing threads – the beginning and end of any piece of work, as well as the many threads in between – is rarely explained, but it is of fundamental importance. Making the first stitch, happy in the knowledge that it is correctly and firmly placed, as well as tidily done, gives much-needed confidence when embarking on a new piece of embroidery.

Threading needles

Threading a needle is something that many people find difficult because of poor eyesight or simply through not knowing the best way to do it. A good way to thread a needle is as follows:
1 Hold the needle in your right hand (left if you are left-handed) and, with your other hand, loop the thread over the point of the needle and pull it tight.
2 Holding this loop firmly between your thumb and first finger, turn the needle around, place the eye over the loop and push it down so that the thread passes through it.

Where to start

Where to start stitching a project is a fundamental question.
• It is always a good idea to work in a continuous flow, rather than starting in several different places and then finding that the work does not join up successfully.
• Where a design requires very dense stitching, it is easiest to start in the centre with the main features and work outwards, as for the Floral Tea Cosy project on page 60.
• For most patterns, but especially for geometric or symmetrical ones, be sure to draw out the whole pattern before starting to stitch (see page 16).

Starting a thread

A thread should be no longer than 50cm (20in). Not only are longer threads uncomfortable for the arm and shoulder, but they can also knot, twist and fray.
• For most embroidery, the neatest way to start is to make a few small stitches, leaving the end of the thread at the front, within the 'flight path' of your stitching – this is the space on the fabric that you intend to cover with the thread presently on your needle. It is important to cover the starting stitches within this section of embroidery to ensure that colours do not overlap, causing the thread of one piece of work to be inadequately masked by another colour.
• Where small starting stitches would not be covered by the embroidery, for instance when working French knots or any exposed stitches, run the thread under a few stitches at the back before starting. Try not to run dark threads into light ones and vice versa, for they may show through. If you are starting where there are no stitches, leave a long thread at the back, then stitch it in when you have worked some embroidery.

Finishing a thread

This can be done in the same two ways as starting a thread.
• If you are continuing in the same colour, make a couple of tiny stitches where they will be covered by the next thread. Leave the end on the top of the work, snipping it off when you reach it.
• If you are using a contrasting colour, turn the work over and run the thread under a few stitches at the back. Never run threads behind the work across an area that is not to be worked: not only can it spoil the tension, but it may show through when you have finished.
  It is important to cut threads off once they have been secured; threads left hanging will tangle and interfere with your stitching.

using this book

Stitches

For ease of reference, the stitches used in this book have been grouped into outline stitches, edging stitches, filling stitches and embellishment stitches. Although the groupings describe the most usual application of each stitch, most are versatile enough to be used in any category. For example, herringbone stitch has been used as an edging stitch in the Red Outline Coverlet on page 27, and as an embellishment stitch to decorate the Crazy Patchwork on page 90; all linear stitches can be sewn in close rows to make them into filling stitches (see the Paisley Sampler Cushion on page 44), while cross stitch could fit into any of the four categories.

Threads

The threads specified for the projects in this book are those that are most widely available. However, you can choose different threads, substitute silks for cottons, use fine pearl cotton in place of coton à broder, and make any changes that may suit your chosen fabric better than the thread specified. To achieve a similar effect to that illustrated, try to select a thread of the same weight. If a different effect is sought, a little experimentation will quickly give you an idea of how different fabrics and threads respond to the stitches used. Do not be afraid to try things out on a spare piece of fabric.

Quantities Every stitcher uses a different amount of thread. So much depends on how close together the stitches are worked, how much thread is used in starting and finishing, and also tension, that the quantities given for each project should be used as a guide only. As many of the pieces are old and the thread quantities therefore not tested, in these cases a best estimate is all that can be given.

Colours The dyeing of commercial embroidery threads is a sophisticated art and there should be no difference in the shade if extra thread is purchased at a later date. Wool is less reliable to colour match, but some variation in shade may enhance rather than detract from the finished embroidery.

Making up

Instructions have been given for making up the embroideries into useful items, but as this is an embroidery, not a sewing, book it is assumed that the reader is familiar with basic sewing skills.

caring for embroidery

Do not be frightened to use your embroidery. If the ends of the embroidery threads have been worked in well, then your finished piece should be robust and you will be able to enjoy it without fear. Many hours of work have gone into making it, so it would be a pity to put it away because it might get damaged. If the work is kept clean, and care is taken with laundering, most embroidery should last a long time, especially if good-quality materials were used to start with.

Using old embroideries

If you have a store of old pieces – pretty but not valuable – that you have inherited, collected, or worked in your childhood, you may be able to make good use of them in different ways from the original intention. On page 68, for example, a tablecloth has been turned into a pretty curtain which shows off the embroidery to better effect than as a tablecloth. Traycloths can be sewn together to make a larger 'patchwork' piece for a bedspread or cushions, and where the fabric is stained or worn but the embroidery is still intact, pieces of the original can be appliquéd on to quilts, pelmets or curtains.

Many old embroideries, especially those from the East, have faded over the years, which adds to their beauty. However, washing them could cause damage. They are best framed and hung on the wall out of direct sunlight.

Washing

Dust and strong sunlight are the main enemies of embroidery. However colourfast the threads are, strong sunlight will eventually bleach out some of the colour, while dust will rot the yarns, especially wool. It is therefore important to keep embroidery clean.

With the exception of canvaswork, most embroidery is washable. If the ends have been properly worked in when starting and finishing (see page 18), and the colours are fast, some larger pieces may even be washed in a machine on a gentle cycle.

Due to environmental concerns, colourfastness is not always as strong as it has been in the past. Colourfast cotton thread is best washed in plenty of hot water, because lukewarm or cold water increases the risk of colour bleeding. Use thoroughly dissolved, mild detergent: avoid 'biological' powders and those with chemicals added for colour brightening and so on.

Do not spin or tumble dry; instead, roll up the wet piece of embroidery in a white towel and press very gently, before hanging up the work to dry. Press the work while it is still just damp, placing it face downwards on thick towelling to prevent the embroidery from flattening. The embroidery threads may not dry as quickly as the fabric, so lay it flat after pressing and leave until it is completely dry.

Never wash canvaswork embroidery (sometimes called tapestry or needlepoint). Washing can shrink the canvas, and also removes the dressing which is added to keep the canvas in shape. In addition, the wool yarn can become matted and fluffy, spoiling its appearance. A thorough steaming should remove dust, but if the embroidery is really dirty, dry cleaning is recommended for best results.

Storing

The best way to store embroidery which will not be displayed for some time is to lay it flat in a drawer, wrapped in acid-free tissue paper. Do not use plastic bags, as the static attracts dust and the textiles will not be able to breathe. Make sure that the pieces are fully covered with tissue, otherwise any protruding edges will yellow, and then lay a piece of sheeting over the top.

Outline embroidery

Outline embroidery is probably one of the oldest forms of the craft, echoing the simplest form of drawing: much of the Bayeux tapestry is wrought in outline, and that is over 900 years old. The popularity of outline work in the mid-1880s was probably the result of patterns being sold which had already been outlined with stitching in one colour. In the USA outline work really caught on, with motifs being published not only in the women's press but in art magazines as well. An American author wrote at the time: 'As the chief beauty of outline work depends upon grace and fidelity of form, it is naturally a craft demanding poetic instinct as well as delicate manipulation.' This is perhaps a distorted view, for the ease and quickness of its execution must have been a major factor in the popularity of the technique, and the mostly naïve quality of the motifs demands little in the way of 'delicate manipulation'.

The work was normally stitched in a single-colour stranded cotton, and

for some reason – probably fashion – this was usually red. Thus the work became known as 'redwork'. Sayings were often incorporated into redwork designs, a common one being worked on pairs of pillowcases, one saying 'I slept and dreamed that life was beauty', and the other 'I woke to find that life was duty'.

22

outline stitches

Outline stitches are the simplest embroidery stitches and outline work is the nearest that embroidery gets to line drawing, for it lends itself to the successful interpretation of simple subjects, even for the novice stitcher. The work is often undertaken in a single colour, giving it a naïve charm in which the motif is more important than the stitching. More ambitious designs can also be executed in outline, using lines of embroidery to shade motifs and introducing a range of colours and textures using different shades and threads. Outline stitches can also be used to fill motifs with interesting texture by working lines of stitching as close together as required. Chain stitch is commonly used in this way, as is stem stitch (see the Paisley Sampler Cushion on page 44).

Running stitch

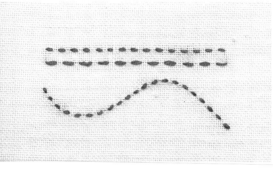

This is one of the most basic of all stitches for any kind of sewing and is used both for decoration and for strengthening. It consists of short stitches running in and out of the fabric in a single line. In embroidery, running stitches give a lightness to small curves, stalks of plants, and any other place where solid lines may be too heavy, the gaps suggesting to the eye that something is there when in fact it is not.

Working from right to left, the

fig 1

needle is taken in and out of the fabric to create a broken line of stitches of a size to suit the embroidery (fig 1).

Laced running stitch

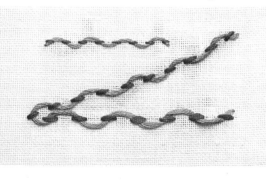

Running stitch can be embellished by lacing with a contrasting colour to form a decorative border, when it is called laced running stitch (fig 2). It is quick and easy to do and looks impressive. The lacing is done once the running stitch is complete, and does not pass through the background fabric. The use of a small, blunt-ended tapestry needle for the lacing enables the needle and thread to pass under rather than pierce the existing embroidery. In the Crazy

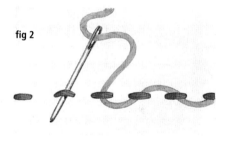

fig 2

Patchwork (see page 90), it has been used to decorate one of the seams between the patches.

Backstitch

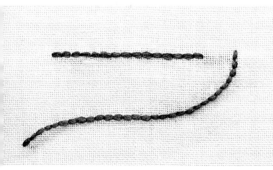

The line produced by backstitch is similar to running stitch, but is continuous, not broken. It is the best stitch for making long, straight lines, as in the Indian Pelmet (see page 64), but can also be used for curves, though it does not curve as smoothly as stem stitch (opposite). It is made by taking a long stitch forward underneath the fabric and a short backward stitch on top, joining with the previous stitch (fig 3).

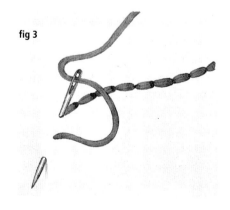

fig 3

Pekinese stitch

This decorative stitch is backstitch laced with looped thread (fig 4). As for laced running stitch (opposite), use a blunt-ended needle for the lacing. It is particularly important to keep an even and fairly loose tension for the best effect. More than one thread can be laced, giving many possibilities for contrasts in colour and texture in what is a very simple stitch.

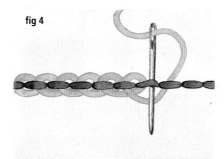

fig 4

Stem stitch

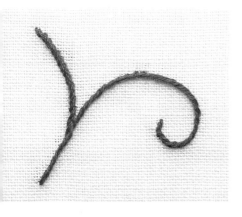

As its name suggests, stem stitch is used for plant stems, but also for outlines where an unbroken, smooth-running line is called for. The stitches overlap one another, and stitching at slightly different angles can give a thicker or thinner line. For a broad, twisted effect, the needle should pierce and emerge through the fabric on either side of the design line (fig 5). For narrow lines of stem stitch, work along the design line itself (fig 6).

1 Start by making a stitch as for running stitch, at the required angle.

2 Bring the needle up half-way back along the previous stitch. Repeat step 2 along the stitching line.

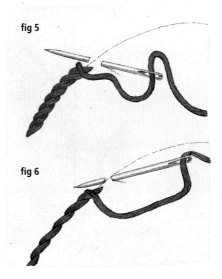

fig 5

fig 6

Chain stitch

Although chain stitch is a simple technique, it is very effective. Worked as an outline stitch it is quick and adaptable. Most Indian wool embroidery (crewel) is worked in chain stitch only, executed using a hook for speed. This is sometimes called 'tambour' work, because the fabric is stretched tight across a hoop – like the surface of a tambourine. The sharply pointed tambour hook is punched through the fabric, picking up the thread from underneath. Early sewing machines worked in the same way, producing chain stitch instead of the familiar straight stitch of today.

There are several versions of chain stitch, but the simplest one is used for the crewelwork on the Crewelwork Pansies (see page 30), worked with an ordinary chenille needle.

1 Bring the thread up through the fabric. Holding the thread down with the left thumb, insert the needle where, or close to where, it emerged. Bring the point out a short distance away in the direction in which the stitches are to lie, looping the thread underneath (fig 7).

2 Pull the thread through and continue the chain in the same way (fig 8).

fig 7

fig 8

25

red outline coverlet

Stitches used
stem stitch (page 25),
French knots (page 76),
herringbone stitch (page 76).

This American embroidery is made up of ninety separate pieces each carrying its own, often rather curious, motif. The simplicity and naïvity of the patterns are what make the coverlet so appealing, providing endless speculation as to why its creator chose to embroider a potato, a bucket, or a piece of cheese alongside the more usual subjects of flowers and animals. Eight of these motifs are illustrated below and overleaf. However, the joy of undertaking a piece like this lies in gathering together designs and symbols that relate to your own life, for it is the individuality of the work that is its most important attribute.

Sometimes these coverlets would be stitched by a number of people, but this appears to be the work of one person, for the stitching is close and regular. The date 1903 is embroidered in one of the squares. The coverlet would make a superb wall hanging (see page 23) and could also double as a tablecloth.

You will need
Cotton sheeting, to create as many squares as required – the pieces on this coverlet measure approximately 21cm (8in) square when finished (seam allowance 2cm/¾ in)
Crewel (embroidery) needle size 5 or 6
Stranded cotton in the colour of your choice

To work the embroidery
1 Draw out your designs on separate squares of paper, using the motifs given here and overleaf, or creating some others of your own. Transfer on to the fabric by any of the methods described on pages 16-17.
2 Using all six strands of thread throughout, embroider the squares separately. Work all the outlines of the motifs in stem stitch and add small details such as flower centres and animal eyes in French knots.

To make up
1 Lay out the squares on a large table or on the floor and change them around until you are satisfied with the configuration.
Machine stitch the squares together into strips. Trim the seams to approximately 1cm (⅜in) and press open.
2 Then sew the strips together, trimming the seams and pressing them open as before. It is important to tack first, so that the squares fit well and do not slip out of place when running through the machine.
3 Oversew the seams with herringbone stitch, which will disguise the joins cleverly as well as securing the raw edges at the back of the coverlet so that they will not fray. On this piece, the outside edges have been turned in twice and secured by herringbone stitch, too, obviating the need for normal hemming

One of the whimsical images on the coverlet is shown here actual size. More motifs to trace and transfer are given overleaf.

A selection of the motifs used on the coverlet, shown actual size. Trace and transfer on to the fabric, adding other images of your choice.

29

crewelwork
pansies

Stitches used
chain stitch (page 25),
stem stitch (page 25),
lazy daisy stitch (page 75).

Reputed to be the favourite flowers of Queen Elizabeth I, pansies are now in vogue once again. With their relatively uniform shape and idiosyncratic petal formation, they make particularly good subjects for simple outline embroidery. The flower colours, too, are distinctive, and their richness is enhanced by the depth of yarn shades that embroidery wool imbues.

Crewelwork – sometimes called Jacobean work, from the embroidered hangings popular in England during the latter part of the seventeenth century – is embroidery executed in wool. It is not clear whether the name comes from the wool or from the art form itself, but the fine two-ply yarn that is used for this kind of embroidery is generally referred to as crewel wool.

Some of the stitchwork in traditional crewel embroidery is extremely ornate and requires skilled workmanship. However, it need not always be so, as quite simple stitches can be used in exactly the same way as embroidery with cotton or silk. These pansies are stitched in chain stitch – which can be used as an outline as well as a filling stitch – and a little stem stitch.

You will need
For the cushion:
50cm (20in) square backing fabric
35cm (14in) zip
Matching sewing thread
45cm (18in) square cushion pad
For the cord trimming (optional):
3 10m (11yd) skeins single-thread tapestry or double knitting wool in toning colour (Prussian blue in the cushion illustrated)
Matching buttonhole thread, or doubled sewing thread
Hand drill with cup hook fixed to bit (optional)
Crewel (embroidery) needle size 2 or 3

For the embroidery:
50cm (20in) square fine evenweave linen twill fabric
Chenille needle size 22
Cardboard or stiff paper, 50cm (20in) square approx
Embroidery wool in either the Appletons or Paterna colours shown on page 33

To work the embroidery
1 Enlarge the pattern given on page 33 to 156% on a photocopier. Transfer the pattern on to the linen twill fabric using method 2 or method 3 described on pages 16–17.
2 Start by stitching the pansies, outlining the shapes with one or more rows of chain stitch in the colours shown in the key given with the pattern. The direction of the stitch is unimportant. Add the flowers on the mug in lazy daisy stitch with stem stitch stems.
3 When the flowers and mug are complete, make a cardboard cut-out 'window' 33cm (13in) square. Place this over the embroidery and, when it is centred to your satisfaction, draw a line around the inside of the square using a pencil. This is the guideline for the embroidered border.
4 Work two rows of chain stitch along this line using the Prussian blue and airforce blue yarns. Add the crosses in chain stitch using pale aqua, starting at

This pansy motif, taken from the main design, shows the actual size of the flower.